NLP Master's 2 in 1 Box Set:

NLP Master's Handbook
NLP Master's Scriptbook

Table of Contents

NLP Master's Handbook

The 21 Neuro Linguistic Programming and Mind Control Techniques that Will Change Your Mind and Life Forever

Introduction

I want to thank you and congratulate you for purchasing the book, *"NLP Masters Handbook"*.

This book contains proven steps and strategies on how to apply the different NLP techniques to improve your life.

In this book, you will learn 21 helpful strategies and NLP techniques that will eventually change your thoughts so that you can change your behaviors. These steps are easy to follow and understand. They are practical ways to practice mind control to increase your productivity, improve your relationship with other people, and to basically live a more productive and happier life.

Thanks again for reading this book, I hope you enjoy it!

Chapter 1 – NLP: Change Your Mindset, Change Your Life Forever

The mind is the most powerful tool mankind was given. NLP (Neuro Linguistic Programming) is a school of psychological techniques for better communication, to help one perform better and make positive changes in one's life. NLP has been applied to a wide array of fields, such as Psychology, Healthcare, Coaching, Sales, Education, Coaching, and Business.

A lot of people have been utilizing NLP to clear out past regrets, release negative behaviors, kick unwanted habits, and to create positive and permanent changes.

Neuro Linguistic Programming

Neuro refers to your nervous system, which includes the brain and the 5 senses. *Linguistic* refers to the verbal and non-verbal languages by which you communicate. *Programming* is the capability to structure your neurological and linguistic systems in order to achieve desired goals.

NLP was developed by John Grinder and Richard Bandler in the early 1970s. These two set out to create changes in people's lives, particularly in human communication. Its fundamentals are straightforward:

- *You have to know what you want.* One of the most important questions NLP wants you to answer is *"What is it that you want, exactly?"* Do you even know what you want out of life? Do you know what you want to do? The nervous system can be a goal-seeking "tool" which helps you to identify what to focus on.

- *Tap into the subconscious mind.* You need to begin with the person you want to influence. It is important to build rapport; it is a process that helps you get the attention and trust of the subconscious mind of another person. In turn, this helps you build relationships with others.

- *Be aware if you are getting what you want.* When you have identified where you want to go, it is imperative to be aware if you are getting to where you want to go. This is where sensory acuity comes into play; or your ability to notice the signs of your progress towards the right direction (or otherwise).

- *Make adjustments as necessary.* When it seems obvious that you are not achieving what you want, you need to become flexible to make the necessary changes so you can finally arrive at a different outcome. You have to have a fixed goal but you also have to be flexible on how you can achieve it.

NLP and CBT

Most people think these two are somewhat similar. NLP provides simple yet powerful methods to change one's behavior and produce positive results with the use of different techniques.

CBT or Cognitive Behavior Therapy also helps change a person's behavior. It can alter how an individual view themselves and the world. The basic principle of CBT is that people are emotionally disturbed by their own thoughts because of an actual event, rather than the event itself. It taps into your cognitive behavior power.

These two teach you to control your thoughts in order to control your feelings and behaviors. Both use mind control to help an individual make changes in their lives.

Why Should You Learn NLP?

Here are just some of the benefits of learning various NLP techniques:

- Helps you to learn mind control
- Helps you develop the power of persuasion through excellent communication skills
- Allows you to help others to achieve the results they want
- Helps you overcome challenges in your personal, business, and social life
- Helps you achieve more success, joy, and happiness in your life

Chapter 2 – Basic NLP Techniques

There are a variety of NLP techniques that you can use for a host of different purposes. Every technique can be used by itself or combined with other techniques in order to create a new mindset that will be able to change your life forever.

Basically, there are 8 commonly recognized techniques:

#1 Anchoring

Anchoring induces a particular frame of mind or an emotion, like happiness, sadness, or relaxation. It often involves a gesture or touch, or something that you can identify as an *anchor* – it's like a "bookmark" for a particular emotion.

How does it work?

Go back to a time when you experienced overwhelming happiness, like when your child was born, when you won an award, or when you received your first paycheck. It could be anything that you have fond memories of.

In your head, think of the events that transpired leading you to that happy moment. Make the images more vivid. Think about how you felt during that time. Create a clear image of that moment and feel the emotions you had back then.

Next, hold your left index and your middle fingers with your right hand. Gently squeeze your fingers twice. As you squeeze them the second time around, recall the image of that happy moment, only this time, making the picture larger and happening close to you. Remember how happy you felt and feel that intense emotion starting to break free as it multiplies.

Describe how you're feeling again and what you were thinking then, do these while you squeeze your fingers again, twice. As you squeeze the second the feelings you described doubles. Let the feeling envelop your whole being. Feel it.

This is anchoring, each time you make squeezing actions to your fingers; you will be transported back to that time of overwhelming happiness. That particular action sends a signal to your brain to associate it with feelings of happiness.

#2 Pattern Interruptions

This NLP technique is more commonly used to store keywords to your listener's subconscious mind. Pattern interruption is best combined with other NLP techniques, particularly anchoring.

What is it?

Pattern interruption lures your listener's inner monologue or pure subconscious train of thought to establish a pattern.

Take this analogy. There is a boy who gets his pet dog to perform all of his movements for him. The boy is your conscious mind, while the dog represents your subconscious mind. The boy (conscious mind) makes all the decisions, and the dog (subconscious mind) performs all the actions that needed to be done.

Here's where the exercise begins. Ask the boy to make a sandwich. The boy then tells the dog to get the bread, slice the cheese, and place it on a plate. The boy then tells the dog to bring the food to a friend sitting right behind the shadow.

So, you ask the boy that you wanted another sandwich, so he gives his dog a similar sequence of command. The pet dog promptly gets the bread and cheese and places it on a plate.

Then, *"slap"* anyone who is near you. Next, slap the boy in the face and instruct him to dance. Before the dog can finish the final command during the sandwich test was interrupted, new commands have been given.

The boy who is the conscious mind, being depicted here as someone who is less clever, forgets that the sandwich is still not "delivered". However, the pet dog has not forgotten about the sandwich. Though the dog has no capacity to speak to the boy, he is thinking when the command for the sandwich will be given. That thought will stay with the dog for quite some time until he is told to fetch that sandwich.

You can easily tell the boy to give you his wallet. It is easy since the boy might ask his pet dog to bring the wallet to you. It is possible that the dog will bring you the wallet.

This is the perfect example of pattern interruption. This example may not work all the time but this particular technique is powerful.

#3 Swish Pattern

The Swish Pattern is used to replace a negative emotion or behavior with a positive and useful one. When this technique is used, you'll need to be creative with your ideas. To put it simply, Swish is the NLP version of the "copy and paste" in computing. You choose several entries on a document that you want to be copied in another document. With Swish, a portion of neurological tag is copied and pasted to cover another tag of a different memory.

How does it work?

Each of the memories you have in your mind has emotions associated with it. Some of these emotions are good and some are bad. This is how the Swish technique words:

Supposing you're a teenager and you've recently moved to a new neighborhood. Classes in your new school will start the next day. How are you feeling about it? Are you worried or anxious because you don't know anybody there? You are nervous about going to a new school; who wouldn't be? However, by nurturing these negative emotions, people tend to assume that you are really like that, so you will be alienated. They will notice that you are nervous so they don't want to associate with you. It's a vicious cycle.

You have come to associate anxiety with the first day at a new and unfamiliar school. It would benefit you more if you associate going to a new school for the first time to excitement instead.

This is the Swish Pattern technique:

You recall a memory from the past and associate it with the feeling of excitement, like going to a party with friends or visiting a theme park. Focus on how you feel, actively thinking about what is about to happen, and create a mental picture of that activity in your mind. This instantly replaces the image of you going to school the following day.

Keep in mind, when you feel that anxiety or worry are about to set in, SWISH! Replace the negative image and go back to a good memory. The principle is to keep on going back to that feeling of overwhelming excitement. Hold on to that feeling. As you maintain that positive emotion, Swish back and forth as quickly as you can between the two images.

#4 Loop Break

This NLP technique is an experimental one. It prompts you to consciously alter a subconscious process. How is it even possible? It "breaks" a looping process by the body to naturally enter the different higher alpha brain states like fear, anxiety, anger, rage, and stress.

Why should you use the Loop Break technique?

You should use the Loop Break technique to help you control your behavior. When you are able to master it, you can help other people to learn to control their own behaviors.

There is always something that triggers your anger. Imagine you are in your car, driving to your next important meeting. You are running late and your travel time is taking too long for comfort. You begin to feel anxious and stressed. When you reach the traffic lights, another car rear-ends your car. It is highly likely that you'll get angry at this time.

It might do you good if you lash out at the person who bumped your car, only it wouldn't do any good, but rather escalate things. This is definitely not productive. The best reaction is to immediately take note of the other car's license plate number.

You are only human and you will get angry and you are likely to end up starting an argument or a shouting match. You will not be able to think straight, thereby screwing your cognitive capability.

You apply Loop Break by counting from one to ten when you feel that you are getting stressed or mad. It's like breaking the momentum so you can regroup. This helps you think straight so you don't act on impulse.

#5 Framing

Framing can be used in combination with other NLP techniques. It is a kind of emotional amplifier or a de-amplifier. It works by rebuilding links in your limbic system, between the hippocampus and the amygdale.

This is a simple yet effective NLP technique. You learn some of the best lessons in life from your bad experiences and memories, both good and bad. These memories are stored and produced in the different areas of the brain. The hippocampus is responsible for the storage and production of memories, while the amygdala is responsible for all of your emotions.

How is it done?

Recall a memory that triggers negative emotions, like losing your job, or getting caught in a traffic jam, or losing your shoe when you were having your car fixed.

Framing edits your emotional response to a particular memory.

So, continuing on with the previous example, you take a memory and reduce the highlight to just one image that represents that particular memory. This image will remain and represent a negative memory.

Now, step back from the memory of a bad interview. If you wish to look at your memories through your own eyes, you need to step back from yourself in that same situation. If you are comfortable to use a third person perspective, you will have to step back further away.

You begin to see your own self in a single image that represents your bad interview. Now, imagine the picture is in black and white. Make it blurry, similar to an old photograph. Now as you hold that photo in your head, put a frame around the photo with a stainless steel frame or a modern wooden frame.

You need to mount the frame on the wall, like in a restaurant or clinic. You can mount different photos and create different lighting fixtures for the "painting".

And then, move on!

How does this make you feel? Do you still feel stressed? This technique should have dampened the feelings. If you are still feeling negatively, you can repeat the process.

Soon, that memory will only become just a picture, and you will eventually learn to detach emotionally from a painful or negative memory. Framing tricks your brain into downplaying any kind of links to the emotions a certain memory may refer to.

#6 Meta Model

This is a therapeutic technique that is helpful in understanding the problems of other people and making them understand those problems better. The Meta Model "deconstructs what the other person is saying in order to uncover the underlying cause of the problem.

When problems arise, the subconscious mind actually knows the solution already. Most of the time, some people don't like the obvious solutions, hence, they continue to try finding what they perceive are better solutions.

#7 Presuppositions

Presupposition makes use of hypnosis. It is language structure which creates un-verbalized assumptions. One can say to you, *"I am never going to that restaurant again!"* The presupposition is that the other person may have gone to that same restaurant before.

Presuppositions are more powerful when used with subtlety. When one is in the suggestible state (confused), your presupposed statement can have a play on words for the other person to believe it.

A perfect example is a promotional statement for a food product: *"It's different? You might even say it is delicious!"* The statement suggests that the food is delicious. Also, there are two tricky presuppositions in this statement. First, it says *"It's different?"* It is presupposing that the food is not like any other. Second, the statement presupposes that you make a statement confirming that *"You might even say it is delicious!"*

This is a marketing tool using a mild form of hypnosis to make you come back for more.

A type of therapy used to treat a number of mental illnesses, DBT or Dialectical Behavior Therapy can be mapped out into the presupposition techniques of NLP. These are four suppositions that can be made:

- People always want to improve.
- People keep on doing the best that they can.
- People should learn new behaviors.
- No individual fails in therapy.

#8 Mirroring

Mirroring is the most commonly used NLP technique. It is simply mimicking the behaviors and gestures of the person you are speaking with. You can copy with subtlety one's speech patterns, their body language, their tempo, pace, tone, pitch, and the volume of their voice, and the specific words they normally repeat.

Is NLP the same as hypnosis?

Hypnosis is a "unique" state of mind wherein it is mindful, relaxed, and highly suggestible. When one is in a state of hypnosis, it is easier to control your brain.

To practice hypnosis, choose a comfortable armchair or bean bag. You are supposed to be in an inclined position. You need someone you can trust, to perform this with you. Hypnosis won't work if you don't trust you hypnotizer. Hypnosis uses positive terminologies to be more effective and it makes use of the power of persuasion to control the mind.

Chapter 3 – Make Changes in Your Life with These Techniques

The basic NLP techniques can be applied to a lot of things. In this chapter, you will learn about some new techniques combining the different basic NLP techniques.

#9 Begin before you begin, wrap up before you wrap up

This is like using hypnotherapy without other people noticing. If you handle sales people and you want them to rake in more sales, you can use this technique during one of your training courses or coaching sessions or even during a sales call with prospective buyers.

After the mandatory introductions, you can say a statement along these lines, *"There are some things that I want to discuss before we begin..."*

And then you start with the session! Some people often build walls every time they are subjected to a training session and the beginning is always the hardest. Before starting formally, you can tell them or your client that you expect to have a grand time as you work with them. You will never actually notice that you have actually started when the "real" session began.

On the other hand, if you have come to the conclusion of a sales pitch or training your sales agent, you can also finish before you can even make a "formal closing remark". You can simply say, *"I guess that's all for the day,"* then get up and leave.

You may also say, *"Oh, there's something I forgot..."* and then begin again. Prepare to be amazed at what can transpire and how many sales you can make before you wrap up.

#10 Take Other People Literally

Take them at face value. Take the things they say as they are. Ever wondered why most people cannot lose weight? It's because when you ask them what they want, they would tell you, *"I want to lose weight."* Taking that literally, the individual wants to lose weight. That person knows that they want to lose weight but ask them again why and you'll get an answer that they aren't sure how and they cannot picture themselves being slim.

Truth is, people don't like losing things; it's how people are. So ask again, *"What happens if you are slim?"* Notice how the other person would light up because they can easily see a mental image of them being thin.

Using the same example, if you want achieve your ideal weight, imagine yourself already thin and doing the things that you want to do.

#11 Be There First

If you don't know where you're going, the journey would be a struggle. You have the power to change your mind. If you want to achieve success, you have to be able to go transition from your current set of circumstances to your desired set of circumstances.

When you want to influence others to achieve the things you have achieved, you have to "infect" them with you positive attitudes. When you go on meditation, you go into a state of calmness, love, happiness, and gratitude. You apply the NLP anchor technique here. Associate success with a happy event and stick to it until you are already in that state.

Being at your destination first is visualization – it helps you "transport" yourself even before you do it.

#12 Gestures are Powerful

Gestures, mannerisms, and other non-verbal forms of communication are powerful. They can say a million different things. You can build rapport with another person by mirroring their gestures. It is the best way to build a good relationship. If you are into sales, you can use this to generate more sales and improve your productivity.

#13 Milton Model

The Milton Model is named after a renowned hypnotist, Milton Erickson. He used the power of verbal hypnosis to generate the results he wanted. He used words that are "artfully vague". For instance, rather than saying, *"Your body feels relaxed",* he says, *"You are beginning to notice sensations in your body,"* and you will start to notice the changes in your body.

You can look at it this way. You are now reading this book because there are things that you want to learn, and you are interested in discovering how you can apply the principles you have learned into practice.

If you read the above statements again, they may sound specific but they aren't. The words merely suggested what you will experience but they are always true for almost anyone.

This technique would help increase your productivity and output.

#14 The Meta Model

The Meta Model is based on the theory that people do not experience direct reality, but they instead experience it through "maps" of reality that they themselves created in their minds. Whenever they are faced with adversity, it does not exist in reality but in the "map" of reality.

You have the power to change your "map" so that you can easily overcome the challenges. You enrich your reality "map" by the power of framing technique and/or the self-anchoring technique. Practice mind control and you change the course of your "map" of reality.

#15 Do Not Hesitate

It is natural for people to hesitate when they find themselves in a situation where they have to decide on something.

Do this exercise. Identify the areas in your life where you are likely to hesitate. Decide that you would like to just go for it now. Choose a business establishment, like a store, shop, or restaurant, and make an absurd request, like ordering something that they do not sell. Keep a straight face, be polite, and do not threaten. Do this twice in a week. Think about the times when you have hesitated in the past and enjoy new responses today.

Why it will work

Your central nervous system is set up to protect you from dangerous situations. From childhood, people are taught to avoid making mistakes. But the truth is making mistakes is important for your growth and learning. The above exercise will help reduce hesitation and boost your confidence level. There are instances where hesitation is important, especially if you will be put in danger, like when crossing a busy street. Keep that in mind.

Chapter 4 – More NLP Applications

#16 Boost Your Confidence

When you have confidence, you are not afraid to take risks. This is how you boost your confidence with NLP.

- Never hold the idea of confidence in fear or awe; you are subconsciously telling yourself that it is difficult to achieve. Instead, believe that you have the power and that you are confident, right this instance.

- See confidence as a golden aura enveloping your whole being. Feel the energy flow through your body.

- While you are feeling the energy all over your body, use the anchoring technique by pressing your left thumb into your left index finger. Recall a memory when you did something and you felt happy and safe while doing it. You may see yourself in your patio, reading your favorite book. What do you see? What do you hear? Create a vivid image. How confident are you? Continue reinforcing this anchor and each time you feel confidence, press on that anchor again. Let the feeling of confidence grow stronger as you do this.

- Then feel being confident in a place where you feel less safe. Reinforce confidence by pressing on your anchor again. Picture yourself being surrounded by the golden aura of confidence as you walk into a group of strangers in a party. You are confident and sure of yourself.

- Now that you have a mental image of yourself as a confident individual, you have created a memory while you are in your confident state. Hold that image and capture it.

- Use your anchor and feel the confidence overflowing. If at first you don't get the results you want, you can always begin again and repeat the process.

When you feel confident, you become more confident. When you appear confident, other people will react to you in a positive way and when they react that way, your confidence is reinforced.

#17 The Power of Dissociation

Neutralize negative emotions and overcome phobias by dissociation.

- Identify the particular emotion you wish to get rid of, like fear of heights, disliking a place, or resentment towards someone.

- Picture yourself being in that situation from beginning to end as an observer.

- Play the same scene in your mind over and over, then fast-forward, and play it backwards.

- Play the movie mentally backwards, and then add a funny music. Do this at least 4 times.

- Lastly, see yourself experiencing the same situation right this moment. Notice how your feelings toward the situation change? If you still feel negatively about it, repeat the process until it completely changes.

#18 Building Rapport

Rapport is an essential yet easy skill to learn. There are a lot of ways to build rapport with another person. You can use subtle mirroring or you can follow their breathing patterns. You can also assess their main sensory perception. This can be done by talking to them and paying attention to the words they use.

One is auditory when words used include: *"I hear you"*, *"She scratched the surface"*, or *"I am listening to you"*.

A person who is more visual uses these: *"I clearly see what you mean"*, *sparkling,* or *dark.*

Someone is kinesthetic with words like: *"Her vibe is pleasant"*, *"I have a really bad feeling about this"*, or *touch,* or *warm.*

Rapport is important if you want to get along with other people, especially if you are into sales or you deal with different kinds of people every day. When you are aware of what the other person's main sensory perception is, you can respond to them accordingly.

#19 Overcome Fears and Phobias

There will always be something that you are afraid of but if a fear of something becomes debilitating, you should try to overcome it. This technique can be used to overcome almost any kind of phobia.

- Isolate the reason why you are afraid of, say flying. It could be experiencing turbulence as a child or you might have watched a movie about a plane crashing.

- Create a short movie in your mind and play it in a cinema. See yourself sitting in front of the screen.

- See the movie on the screen. Don't push the play button yet.

- Continue to picture the movie on the screen and see it in black and white. Now, make the screen blurry.

- Make the image for the movie smaller, but make sure that it is still visible on the screen, but occupying only half of the entire screen.

- Lastly, turn off the sound for the movie and replace it with loud, happy music.

- Before pushing play, recall the time when you were confident about yourself, like passing an exam or successfully graduating from school. Magnify the feeling you felt during this time. Let that feeling engulf your whole being, then watch the short movie.

- At the end of the movie, congratulate yourself. You got through. You survived. There is no point to being afraid anymore.

- Put the movie back in full screen and full color. Watch it backwards in fast rewind motion. See that it is over in just a few seconds.

- How do you feel after watching it in a fast rewind manner? If you are still afraid, repeat the steps.

Techniques used are framing, swish, and anchoring.

#20 Quit Smoking with NLP Techniques

You might have tried meditation or other Zen methods but you still cannot quit smoking. Hypnosis and NLP might be able to help you finally kick this unhealthy habit.

- Set a negative anchor. Think of the time when you wanted to quit smoking. Take three instances when you strongly wished you were not smoking, like loved ones, social occasions, or when you got sick because of smoking. Play them over and over in your mind as you press your left thumb knuckle onto a hard surface, like a table. Associate this feeling with these thoughts: cigarette tar forms in your lungs causing you to cough incessantly; tar doesn't smell good, causing bad breath; and see yourself getting hospitalized because of smoking.

- Reinforce that anchor and vividly see yourself getting sick as you continue to press your left thumb knuckle on your desk. Focus on the bad effects of smoking.

- Frame the anchor. Make a clear image of the ill effects of smoking. Sense the associated smells and be aware of the feelings associated with them. Reinforce the anchor by continuously pressing your thumb on your desk. Play the video in your mind, repeatedly. Make smoking a painful event.

- Break the cycle. Is there something in your head that tells you to light a cigarette? Do you crave its taste? Whenever you feel the urge, think about the film about the negative effects of smoking. Focus on the negatives. Take a deep breath of fresh air. Feel the clean air flowing into your body. As you take another deep breath, think about your family and the years that you still have with them. When you take another deep breath, think of that one reason for you to quit smoking. It could be health.

- Focus on the reasons why you want to quit and create an image in your mind. Repeat them over and over.

#21 Effective Goal Setting

Do you want to succeed? You have to learn how to effectively create a goal.

- Declare your goal using positive words. What do you want? Where would you want to be in 5 years? State your goal(s) positively. You may use *to buy your dream house in 5 years* or *purchase a luxury car*.

- Specify your goal using sensory based terminologies. What do you expect to see (or hear, feel, etc.) when you achieve your goal? What steps did you have to create to achieve your goal?

- Specify your goal in a compelling way. Does it inspire you to work hard for it?

- Ensure that the goal you set will benefit yourself and the people around you. Do not create a goal that will compromise your principles and jeopardize your life and your loved ones' lives.

- Make a goal that is measurable and achievable.

- Establish if you can easily initiate and act on the plans of action.

- Know the resources that you need to achieve that goal.

- Take note of your progress. Make it one goal at a time.

If these NLP techniques are done properly, expect to notice changes in all areas of your life. Keep in mind that they may be effective but you still have to perform the needed actions to ensure their success.

Conclusion

Thank you again for reading this book!

I hope this book was able to help you to make changes in your thoughts to initiate changes in your life.

The next step is to begin applying the things you have learned from this book. Don't forget to share what you've learned with your family and friends.

Thank you and good luck!

NLP Master's Scriptbook

The 24 Neuro Linguistic Programming & Mind Control Scripts That Will Maximize Your Potential and Help You Succeed in Anything

Introduction

Thank you for reading the book, *"NLP Master's Scriptbook"*.

Here you'll find 24 NLP and mind control scripts that can help improve your life drastically by maximizing your potential and helping you succeed in anything that you put your mind to. The scripts provided can serve as guides so that you can make your own script, which will be better suited to your specific needs and goals.

Everything starts from the mind; when you begin to think big, expect big things to happen in your life. It's not rocket science; when you are in control of your mind, you are in control of your life. The key to the success of the NLP scripts is in creating a positive mindset and maintaining that mindset through consistent use and practice of the scripts provided. Ultimately, only you can change the situations that you find yourself in, and only you can decide to take action on a day-to-day basis.

Therapists know the power of mind use therapies like CBT, DBT, and hypnotherapy to make a positive and lasting impact in the lives of their patients. NLP isn't just some "psycho-babble" as the critics would have you believe. This is tried and true science and has been proven to be effective over and over again.

There's no denying that change is inevitable. After all, it is the very nature of life. All you have to do is to embrace it. Make that change now!

I hope you enjoy and learn a lot from this book, but remember; only you can choose to take action and implement these scripts into your daily life. I can show you the door, but you must walk through it.

Good luck!

1. You Deserve Success

Today, you find yourself standing at a fork in the road. What do you choose – the path to success or the path to failure? Well, if you picked the former, don't expect a worry-free ride. But that's okay because challenges are there to make success sweeter.

Important note – Italicized lines enclosed in quotation marks are to be recited.

Now, we begin by learning a meditation technique to achieve Zen.

- Sit somewhere comfortable.

- Close your eyes. Take deep, slow breaths and begin counting from 10 to 1.

  - 10…Allow your body to relax.

  - 9…Begin to let go.

  - 8…See the number as you continue to go into relaxation.

  - 7…See it clearly and let go.

  - 6…You are relaxing deeply now.

  - 5…Take your time – deeper and deeper, your body is relaxed.

- o   4...Rid the mind of all outside noises.

- o   3...See the number and let it all go.

- o   2...You are going deeper and deeper.

- o   1...Finally, you are in deep relaxation.

- You are now in a state where your mind absorbs anything.

- See yourself on an imaginary screen in front of you. You see a successful person who is grateful for everything.

- You remain positive despite the challenges and your confidence level is high. You are in control of your own thoughts because you are aware that your thoughts will become your reality.

- You remain true to your goal. You know exactly what it is you want and you continue to see it clearly in your mind.

- *"I cannot wait to achieve my goals. I act and behave as a successful person does. I deserve success. I am open to change and I embrace it. My time has come!"*

- In a few moments, you will get out of this hypnotic state, 1, 2, 3, 4, 5.

- Your eyes begin to open and you feel better than before.

2. You Have the Power to Change

This is how you let go of the past so that you can have control over your future by effecting change in your life in the present moment.

- Begin by doing deep breathing techniques. Your muscles begin to relax. Your mind and body begins to relax, as your eyes grow heavy with every deep breath you take.

- See yourself wander to a stream. The water is clean and there are trees all around. This is a tranquil and serene place.

- You see yourself lying in the water and your body begins to float. Your entire weight is being supported by the water beneath you.

- *"I am safe. I am protected."*

- You hear the sounds of the waterfall as it comes into full view, and you see clear water splashing down.

- You go under the waterfall and you feel lighter than ever. You begin to see lights of different colors and they enter your skin. They are healing you right this moment. The water and the light are washing away and healing all the pains and disappointments of the past. You begin to let go.

- You begin to focus on what you have in front of you – a stream of water ready to take that journey with you.

- The waterfall lets you focus on the present moment. *"I believe that everything I do today will directly influence my future, so I will think only of positive thoughts."*

- *"I am now in control of my life."*

- As you emerge from the water, you are a different person. You begin to feel the power and energy that will drive you onward. You now have the power to take on your present to ensure that you have a better future.

3. Overcome the Fear of Failure

You will never become successful if you continuously nurture your fear of failure. This fear exists only in your mind and you can use your mind to overcome it. Don't let fear keep you from achieving what you are supposed to achieve. Release all your fears and begin to feel free to succeed.

- Take a deep breath. With each deep breath, your body begins to relax. Let go of the tension in your muscles.

- Now, close your eyes and continue to breathe deeply and slowly as possible. Your mind and body is now relaxed.

- See yourself wandering in an empty street. You look around and the street is empty. As you continue to walk, you notice how the structures around you look neglected. You see blank windows. Buildings have no signs. The place looks abandoned. It's a dark place.

- You look ahead and you cannot see the end of the road.

- The wind blows up the dust on the street. There's no place to hide and you are scared. You just stand there and wonder how you even got there.

- Instead of being afraid, you begin to think of happy thoughts as you sit. You begin to think about how happy you were when your mom first bought you your toy car. Then you remember how amazed you were when you first went to your first magic show.

- You begin to think only positive thoughts and then you begin to open your eyes. You are still there in the middle of an empty and dusty street, but this time you are not afraid.

- You know that this is not the destination you want, and it's not the destination you deserve. So you begin to walk straight ahead.

- You remain focused straight ahead. You push aside the fear. You continue to walk and as you quiet down your heavily beating heart with positive thoughts, you begin to see a bright new horizon.

- Slowly, you see yourself entering a different street – where everything is bright and sunny. You begin to see people walking, talking, and laughing. You look around and see offices and buildings bustling with people.

- You know this is where you should be and you are not afraid anymore.

4. Patience is a Virtue

Everything is a process. You need to work for your success. It doesn't happen overnight. Still, some people do not have the patience to wait.

- Get into the process of deep relaxation and breathing.

- *"I am patient and I understand that only the present exists. The concepts of tomorrow and the past remain elusive."*

- *"I am patient. I let go of the past because it can never be relived. The future is still non-existent so I don't have to worry about it. The only thing that matters is what happens today."*

- *"I am patiently developing and creating my future with what I do and think today. In the meantime, I am enjoying every moment. There is no reason to be worried about the future."*

- *"I am patiently living in the present! Everything will come together, eventually!"*

5. Feel Good about Yourself

When you feel good, you stay positive, and that's what you need if you want to attract success in your life.

- See yourself in a giant movie screen in front of you. See yourself clearly – the color of your clothes, your facial expression, what you are doing, and the scenery behind you. Make the details as vivid as possible.

- Now, imagine that your "screen self" is feeling good right at that moment. See the person you see on screen and your real self merging – now you have allowed your "real self" to feel good too.

- *"I deserve to feel good. I deserve this."*

- *"I feel wonderful. I have never been this happy. I am healthy. I feel relaxed. I feel calm. I am happy!"*

- Now, each time you feel down because of disappointments or stress you should go back to imagining yourself on the screen feeling good and merge your "two selves" together.

6. Boosting Confidence

It is easy to lose confidence when failures come but you can help yourself get past that. Each time you need a confidence boost, breathe deeply and let your imagination fly.

- Allow your mind to relax by taking slow deep breaths. Allow your body to let go of the tension and anxiety.

- See yourself on a movie screen in front of you. You have full control of your screen self.

- Imagine yourself in a situation where you want to feel more confident. See yourself clearly. For instance, you want to be confident when you pitch a project proposal to a group of potential clients. See yourself in front of the client. See the images clearly – what you are wearing, where you are standing, what you are doing, how your audience is reacting, and how they interact with you. Make the images as vivid as possible.

- *"I am okay. I am doing fine. I can nail this. I feel good about myself. I am confident of the work I've done for this project."*

- Reflect on what you've seen on the screen. Imagine it happening for real. Congratulate yourself for a job well done.

- *"I am a new person. I deserve to be happy. I deserve all the accolades. I am confident in my skills and in what I am capable of. I am great!"*

7. Staying Positive

It is sometimes hard to stay positive when faced with day-to-day challenges. Staying focused on positive thoughts is an integral part of each of the scripts in this book, but it can be difficult.

Understanding how the mind works is the key. If your body is a vessel, your mind is the captain that runs the ship. The thoughts that you focus on will determine where the ship will go. If you feed your mind with negativity, then you'll end up negative and afraid. If you nurture positivity, then you'll end up positive and happy. So what do you choose?

- Imagine your mind is a car that is running on empty. You need fuel to be able to go to your destination. Feeding your mind with positive fuel would help it work in a positive manner.

- Read thought-enlightening books. Watch a feel good movie or TV program. Listen to good music. Meditate. Go outdoors and bask in the sun. Play with kids or with your pet.

- Think about the things that make you happy – the sound of the laughter of your child, or maybe the taste of cake or ice cream – anything that gives you a reminder of being happy.

- *"It is a good day! I am happy. I think only positive thoughts. I feel great!"* Fuel your mind with positive words.

- Keep looking for things to feel positive about. Associate yourself with positive people. Bring with you a small book of positive quotes.

- *"I am happy and I feel great!"*

8. Creating an "Organized" Environment

Your mind is clear when you are organized and focused.

- Imagine yourself entering a home that is well organized – where everything has a place, where everything has a purpose, whether to add beauty or functionality.

- Hear yourself saying, *"This is exactly who I am. I am an organized person. I am capable of creating an environment similar to this."*

- You continue to explore the home and you feel the calmness it brings. *"I am an organized person and my environment reflects my own beauty and simplicity. I joyfully commit to set at least half an hour every day creating a calm and tranquil environment.*

9. When You Feel You Don't Matter

Some people belittle themselves, especially when they are poor or have no education. They feel that there's nothing they can do to improve their lives. If sometimes you feel that you do not matter, think again and let this exercise help you understand that you are worthy – just like everyone else.

Have you ever looked at the stars at night and wondered how they look all the same yet scientists have a name for some of them? Each one is different; like every human being is different. No two persons are the same; even twins have their differences.

- *"I am unique. There is no one exactly like me. I'm perfect just the way I am. I may have flaws but I also have my own strengths."*

- When people look down on you, it is a reflection of their behavior. Don't ever look down on yourself.

- If you remain poor, that is because you don't want to give yourself a fighting chance to improve your life.

- *"I have my own skills and I am using them to improve my own life."*

10. When You Need to Re-Energize

Your daily grind can drain you. It is important that you re-energize so you can get back to working your full potential again.

- Imagine walking on a beautiful sandy beach with pristine waters. Now as you walk further, you notice that it's almost sunset and you have reached a beautiful lagoon. As you watch the sun going down into the water, marvel at its beauty.

- Feel the water in the lagoon as you go in. The water is just waist deep and you sit down, and then you find yourself floating immediately.

- Feel yourself letting go as you float freely and feel your body begin to relax.

- You are now looking into the sky. It is nightfall now and the stars are shining brightly. The Milky Way comes into full view and you begin to feel your body floating away into the Milky Way. As you float deeper into the galaxy, you begin to feel energized and completely relaxed.

- You begin to float back into the lagoon. You are now feeling the cold water. You see yourself standing up and you feel rejuvenated.

- You walk back into the beach feeling fully rested.

- Looking back into the lagoon, you know that you can always go back to this place whenever you need to recharge.

11. When You Need to Rise above Challenges

Consider yourself half dead if you don't encounter the ups and downs of life. You can never fully appreciate the ups if you have not conquered the downs. When you face adversities and challenges, you have to fight through them and not fall so far into despair that you give up.

- See yourself in a situation with someone that you have had difficulty working with. Think about just one instance that you had a disagreement with him or her. If there are several people and situations that you can think of, set those aside for now. Just focus on one person and one event in each session.

- Imagine the scene unfolding – the person comes up to you and suddenly begins to bicker. As the person continues to berate you, imagine him/her continuously shrinking until he/she is about three inches tall. As he/she shrinks, his/her voice gradually becomes more and more inaudible.

- As the other person keeps on shrinking, see yourself growing taller and taller until you are standing above them. You have become so tall that your head almost reaches the clouds. Feel the fluffy clouds around you and see how blue the sky is.

- *"I feel wonderful. I can rise above it all. I am bigger than anybody who puts me down. I am bigger than my problems. I am bigger than any difficult situation I have to face."*

- You have taken control of the situation. You realize that you can do it and you will do it.

12. How to Fight Stress

While there may be many things to think of and worry about, you don't need to succumb to stress.

- *"Everything is working out fine. I remain calm. I remain positive."*

- Do you notice how it feels good to stay positive despite facing a mammoth of a task or a challenging situation? When you remain positive, you stay in control. You remain focused on the task at hand.

- When you continue to have a positive attitude, you can think clearly and you see the most appropriate solutions to every problem.

- *"I know that I can work through this. I am easily finding the solutions to my problems. I know exactly what to do; there is no reason to worry."*

- Focus on your breathing as you say these positive words. Handle stress by thinking positively and practicing deep breathing techniques.

- Notice how good that feels? Notice how a positive attitude can melt away stress and anxiety?

- Stay positive and melt the stress away.

13. Be More Open to Receiving All the Good Things

It is okay to expect only the good things in life. When you remain positive, you will attract more positivity into your life. Be open. You're like a newly-purchased computer – one that's still in the process of getting all essential programs installed.

- Think about positive thoughts. Reject thoughts of poverty, sickness, and sadness; instead replace them with thoughts about freely receiving abundance, good health, and happiness.

- It is okay to desire to be happy and to be wealthy.

- *"I am open to the abundance that the universe has to offer. I am open to happiness. I am open to good health."*

- *"I attract wealth easily. I am a money magnet. I remain healthy and happy."*

- *"Money, good health, and happiness are flowing freely into my life and I am giving it out to the world."*

14. How to be Grateful

Having the attitude of gratitude keeps the good things coming in. When you remain thankful for all the things that you receive, they will keep on coming.

- See yourself up on a mountain. Look at the magnificent view. Look at the beauty of the world around you. You are atop the highest peak and clouds are all over. You step onto one of the fluffy clouds and it takes you to a wonderful place where you find peace and complete calmness.

- As the cloud transports you, feel your body relaxing deeply. You are now sinking into the calmness of the beautiful place the cloud has brought you.

- You feel the gentle breeze and the warmth of the sun on your skin.

- *"I am grateful for this beautiful place. I am grateful for having been able to experience this. I am grateful for being in this place right now. I am grateful for everything that I see around me. I am grateful for the peace and tranquility I am experiencing right now."*

- As you marvel at nature's beauty, think about the good things that you have in your life. Think about your family, your work, your business, your friends, your house, your car, and all the good things you can think of.

- *"I am grateful for the gift of life. I am thankful for my family."* As you go on enumerating the wonderful things you have in your life, feel it into your being. Recite everything that you are most thankful for. Feel the joy of being grateful for everything that you have in your life.

15. Taking Charge of Your Weight

Part of feeling good is looking good, plus, it is never healthy to be overweight. If you want to lead a healthy lifestyle, you have to begin with losing weight.

- Give yourself a pat on the shoulder for finally deciding to change your life and your physical appearance.

- Picture yourself walking into the park in your neighborhood. There are other people all around and they cannot help but look admiringly at you. Your friends take notice of how great you look.

- As you continue to walk, you feel lighter and you're bursting with energy. You feel wonderful in your new body. As you go back to the house, you catch a glimpse of yourself in a glass window.

- *"I am fit. I am healthy. I love the way my body looks now. I am vibrant. I am happy. I feel great!"*

- From this moment forward, you have to commit yourself to changing your eating habits and becoming more physically active.

16. Kicking the Bad Habits

If you want to improve your life, you have to learn to stop your bad habits. For instance, if you wish to lead a healthy lifestyle, you have to quit smoking.

- Practice deep and slow breathing until your whole body is relaxed.

- Think about the bad habit that you want to break. If there are several habits that you want to overcome, do it one a time. If you want to quit smoking, do it first.

- *"I will quit smoking starting today. I want to lead a healthy lifestyle. I am positive that I will kick this habit in no time."*

- See yourself throwing away packs of cigarettes in your drawer.

- *"I am better off without these. I am healthy. I am stronger. I am happier! I feel great!"*

17. Overcoming Procrastination

Some people think that they have unlimited time to complete a project of meet a deadline so they slack away until they have to cram. Overcome procrastination and avoid stressing out cramming to complete a project.

- For fear of failing or being criticized, some people tend to put off doing things until it is the "best time". Overcome this fear by thinking about your abilities. Find confidence. You were assigned that project because your boss knows you can do it.

- Think about the time that you first submitted a project and your boss commended you for it.

- Allow your mind to see you in your daily routine. See yourself determined to finish the task at hand. Reframe your mind. Take control.

- *"I am finishing this project now. I have all the things that I need to finish this now. I will not slack off and I will not disappoint my boss. I am good at what I do. I am never late. I am great!"*

- You have the power to change. Change your frame of mind. Do it now!

18. Letting Go of Your Emotions

There are moments when you become too emotional for your own good, especially during a time when you need to firmly decide on something.

- Practice deep and slow breathing. Feel your body relaxing.

- Be aware of your feelings. Think about the issue at hand. You need to decide on something but you cannot think objectively because your good judgment is being clouded by your emotions.

- Continue to relax but get in touch with that feeling.

- *"I am afraid of making the wrong decision."*

- Acknowledge that feeling.

- Now see yourself drifting into a dark room, bringing that negative emotion with you. See yourself go deeper and deeper into the dark. Understand why you are feeling that way. Search within you to find the source of that fear.

- Then, feel your body floating away from the dark room but leaving the negative emotion behind. Feel your body going into a brighter room feeling more relaxed.

- You can see clearly now. You have just released that negative emotion of fear and you are now ready to make a huge decision.

- *"I am calm! I am relaxed. I feel great!"*

19. Mastering the Art of Negotiation

If you want to effectively communicate and negotiate with other people, you need a lot of patience and understanding. In meetings and discussions, it is inevitable to have disagreements but neither side is necessarily right or wrong. They just have their own beliefs. You have the power to rise above any kind of situation. Let them speak and do not force your ideas on other people. Understand and listen. Have an open mind.

- *"I am open to the opinion of others. I understand where they are coming from and I am willing to listen. I already know my ideas and it's time to learn theirs."*

- "Negotiate" a solution that everyone can work with, act from a position of power – the power of knowledge. Ask questions and understand their views. When you keep asking questions, you take control.

- When they are finished speaking, repeat what they said to make sure that you understood and then share your ideas, taking into consideration their ideas.

- You are still in control but you have made other people believe that they, too, have a say in the decision-making.

- Having been able to exercise patience and being open-minded, you can negotiate from the "position of knowledge". This is how you can sway other people to implement your ideas without being overbearing. You are in control. Be patient.

20. Improving Your Productivity

When you are productive, you get more work done, thus your superiors will continue to trust you with projects. You have to learn to shut off distractions so you remain focused on the task at hand.

- When you have reached a state of relaxation, see yourself on your desk working on a project.

- See yourself focused, yet happy and calm.

- *"I am productive. Though I have tons of work to do, I will not panic; I'll do things one at a time until I've completed them all. I start with the most difficult and important one. I will stop for short breaks but I won't let my mind get distracted. I am happily working on my tasks and I feel good about it."*

21. Letting Go of Self-Criticism

It is common for most people to be highly critical of themselves. But you have to understand that nobody's perfect and everyone makes mistakes. You have to learn from your mistakes and then move on.

- Close your eyes and go back to a time when you were overly critical of something wrong that you did. Instead of beating yourself up for making a mistake, accept it and learn from it; and then let it go.

- Now, see yourself taking on a new project and completing it without a hitch.

- Let go of self-criticism; embrace your weaknesses and enhance your strengths.

- *"I am positive. I made a mistake but I have learned from it and now I am moving on."*

22. Accomplishing Your Goals

Believe that you can achieve anything. You cannot set limitations on what you can do.

- Focus on your goals. You should never lose sight of your hopes and dreams.

- When you remain focused, you won't settle for anything less.

- Change your frame of mind and stay positive.

- *"By this time next year, I have already built my dream house. My family and I are living comfortably in that dream house."*

- *"I can accomplish anything I set my mind into. I am a winner and I am worthy of getting everything this universe has to offer. I may fail but I will rise again. I will use the challenges that come my way as stepping stones to achieving my goals."*

- Beginning today, you have to believe that you can achieve anything.

23. To Be More Assertive

Your ideas matter; don't let people tell you otherwise.

- Just because you are not the boss, does not mean your ideas don't matter. Just because you are not well educated, does not mean you cannot accomplish anything.

- Don't belittle yourself. If you do, you will never accomplish anything. Always give 100% when you perform your job, not because you are somebody important, but because you are, you and you are capable.

- *"I am capable like everybody else. I am never afraid of voicing out my opinions and sharing my ideas. I am excited to learn new things. I impress people with what I can do. I am a leader!"*

24. Overcoming a Fear of Public Speaking

One of the most common phobias is the fear of speaking in public. People fail because they let fear take the better of them. It is natural to feel nervous every time you need to speak in public. However, if you did the necessary readings and preparations, there is no point in being anxious. These words will also help:

- *"I am confident in my abilities. I believe in myself. People love me."*

- *"People find me warm and friendly. They are drawn to me. They respond to me because I am a person with integrity. They enjoy my company."*

- *"When I get up and speak in front of people, they feel my warmth and they listen to me. I stand in front of people, poised and calm. I speak spontaneously. I am confident with the way I deliver my lines. When I speak, people listen because I speak with authority and conviction."*

Conclusion

Thank you for reading this book.

I hope you have taken the scripts to heart; it will completely turn your life around.

The challenge now is to practice what you have learned and don't forget to share it with your family and friends.

Thank you and good luck!

Don't miss the next book in the series!

"Emotional Intelligence Handbook: Your Quick Start Guide For Making Friends With Emotional Intelligence And Raising Your EQ"

Keep reading for a sneak peek!

Chapter 2: Raising your Emotional Intelligence

Each and every piece of information that the human brain receives and processes passes through any of the five senses: sight, smell, hearing, taste and touch. All of these senses are tied with an individual's emotions, so when you become too tense or emotive, impulse takes control of your ability to think clearly and behave appropriately.

If you are not able to control your own emotions, then you will constantly behave according to your fight-or-flight response, which can be detrimental not only to your health but also to your social relationships with those around you.

Why Raise your Emotional Intelligence?

It is important for you to raise your emotional intelligence so you can better control and balance your emotions in your own terms. When you are emotionally intelligent and your emotions are well-balanced, you can make more rational decisions and responses in your everyday interaction with people. This will lead to better relationships, better health and a happy and successful life as a whole.

In order to raise your emotional intelligence, you will need to be the master of your emotions and not the other way around. For most people, their emotions are their master. How many times have you heard people say that they are sorry because they could not control their emotions? They have done or said something wrong or hurtful to others, only to end up apologizing because they "could not control" their feelings.

However, mastering one's own emotions is easier said than done. One has to develop the proper skills needed to do so.

Skills Needed to Raise Emotional Intelligence

Raising your emotional intelligence and mastering your own emotions will require you to learn a few basic skills. They are discussed in detail below:

Skill#1: The capacity to decrease stress right away.

Stress is your great saboteur when it comes to dealing with your emotions. It is what gets in the way of rational thinking and what hinders appropriate behavior and wise responses. So learning how to block stress at once is essential to mastering your emotions.

There are three actions that you must constantly practice to learn the skill of reducing stress right in the heat of the moment. They are as follows:

- Recognize what stress feels like for you. How does your body feel when anxious? Does your heart palpitate? Do sweat beads line up your forehead? Do you tend to be confused when tensed? Or do you become temporarily paralyzed when under pressure? Be aware of these things.

- Determine your unique reaction to stress. Everyone responds to stress differently so you should find out your own and become acquainted with it. Being conscious of your own stress reactions will help you manage it when it occurs. For example, if you lean towards being confused when stressed, then you can manage it by slowing down, sitting still for a moment and taking some deep breaths.

- Find out which stress-reliever works best for you. There are many actions that you can do to reduce stress instantly, such as deep breathing, meditation, praying, listening to soothing music or walking outside for a while. However, you have to first figure out the first two items above to be able to know what will be effective to you personally.

Skill#2: The capacity to pinpoint your own emotions and stop them from overpowering you.

Successfully pinpointing your emotions and having constant control over them requires you to have a moment-by-moment consciousness of it. Develop a strong connection between you and your emotions and understand how they affect your mind and behavior. Here are some tips on how to do that:

- Build your self-esteem. Low self-confidence disconnects you from your emotions, which gives them power over you.

- Be comfortable with your emotions. Do not feel bad whenever you experience extreme emotions such as anger, bliss, sorrow or fright. Be familiar with it and get to know it. The more that you try to push them away, the more that they can control you. This is because in reality, you cannot actually get rid of them because they are a part of you.

- When sudden sharp emotions emerge, take it as an opportunity to practice Skill#2.

Make sure you check out the rest of this book on Amazon by visiting: **http://www.books4everyone.com/eq**